HER NAME WAS
Yennenga

A Symbol of determination and courage

ANITA KANE

BALBOA.PRESS

A DIVISION OF HAY HOUSE

Balboa Press books may be ordered through booksellers or by contacting:

Balboa Press
A Division of Hay House
1663 Liberty Drive
Bloomington, IN 47403
www.balboapress.com
844-682-1282

Illustrations: André Daniel TAPSOBA
Animated Film Illustrator
Tel: (+226) 78 25 92 43
(+226) 60 19 19 02
email: andrelido01@yahoo.fr

Print information available on the last page.

ISBN: 979-8-7652-2680-3 (sc)
ISBN: 979-8-7652-2682-7 (hc)
ISBN: 979-8-7652-2681-0 (e)

Library of Congress Control Number: 2022906005

Balboa Press rev. date: 04/14/2022

ACKNOWLEDGMENTS

I thank all the people in Burkina Faso and in Canada who contributed to making this book a success.

I dedicate this book to Maëlle Banvie, Danielle Rayanna, and Maïmouna Anita.
Like Yennenga, dare to have big dreams and have the courage to make those dreams a reality.
Be ambassadors of African pride and do so with grace, elegance, and humility.
With love,
Auntie Anita

CONTENTS

PROLOGUE

History cannot give us a program for the future,
but it can give us a fuller understanding of
ourselves, and of our common humanity, so
that we can better face the future.

— Robert Penn Warren,
The Legacy of the Civil War

For a very long time, it was a fundamental belief that men are
superior to women. Even today, this belief persists in some
African societies. The story of Princess Yennenga challenges
this idea and invites reconsideration of what we really believe
about the genders.

The legend of Yennenga is very popular in Burkina Faso, a
West African country whose name in the local language means
"country of people of integrity." Very early on, little girls learn
about Yennenga, either at school for those lucky enough to be
able to attend, or through their parents or grandparents.

Legends and myths are fundamental elements of African
literature that allow us to understand history in all its

complexity. Although it is difficult to place in a specific time frame the history of this princess from the Mossi ethnic group, most narrations state that Yennenga was born between the tenth and fifteenth centuries and that she was the only daughter of King Nedega and Queen Napoko.

Knowledge of the legend of Yennenga comes from the Mossi oral tradition—from chronological narratives transmitted from generation to generation by griots—and from the writings of explorers, colonizers, and researchers who conducted surveys among the Mossi population in the past.

There are several versions of the history of Yennenga which differ depending on the interpretation of the past and the origin of the narrator. However, the version recounted in this book is based on the dominant oral tradition, which is generally accepted by all with regard to the basic events of the story. Opinions differ on certain details—especially on the disappearance of the princess. Some historians report that Yennenga's horse was carried away during an offensive and got lost in the forest. Others maintain that the princess deliberately left the kingdom to escape the authority of her father. However, everyone agrees that, after a long ride, the princess found herself in the middle of a vast clearing where her exhausted horse finally stopped.

Generally, the story of Princess Yennenga is told to relate the origins of the Mossi Empire.

Because of the values that the author wishes to convey, some characters and details are pure creations of the author's imagination, but they find their origin in traditional Mossi societies. This is the case, for example, with the character of the old lady Tipgo, who plays an important role in the spiritual education of the princess. Indeed, Tipgo, whose character demonstrates that life is influenced by mysterious forces taught Yennenga not to ignore the inner voice that spoke to her; she taught her to appreciate the presence of the "beings of light" that protected and guided her. As a result of Tipgo's teachings, the young princess learned to detect the clues that appeared in the course of her journey, even if they did not seem to form a clear message.

Also, the illustrations presented are interpretations and are not intended to accurately represent the architecture, ornaments, characters, and hairstyles of this era.

Although there are many variations of the story of Yennenga, the complete story goes beyond legend and myth. Princess Yennenga did exist, and her story represents a significant part of the historical heritage of Burkina Faso and of Africa in general.

Every legend has a basis in reality. With a little imagination—from the author and the reader—the unique existence and incredible story of Yennenga comes alive in this account.

Beyond the creation of the Mossi Kingdom, there are several lessons to be learned from the life of Princess Yennenga. Her story is also an example of compassion, forgiveness, love, and above all, the courage and determination of a woman who emancipates herself from some aspects of patriarchal traditions.

This book offers an interpretation of Yennenga's story that

highlights basic and fundamental human values which remain relevant and important even in the twenty-first century.

Yennenga's grave in Gambaga, a town in what is now the Republic of Ghana in Africa, is a place of pilgrimage and reverence. And that is where the story of Yennenga begins....

Chapter 1

Behind a Great Kingdom
Is a Great King

Great leaders are not defined by the absence of
weakness, but rather by the presence of clear
strengths.
—John Zenger, *The Handbook for Leaders: 24
Lessons for Extraordinary Leadership*

Around the year 1100, in the town of Gambaga in the Kingdom
of Dagomba, there lived a great king called Nedega. Nowadays,
this kingdom is located in a territory bordering Ghana and
Burkina Faso, in West Africa.

Nedega was the leader of the Dagomba Kingdom because he
had succeeded in uniting the peoples of the northeastern Niger
Delta: The Dagomba, the Mamproussi, and the Nankana.

The Dagomba Kingdom was strong and prosperous, which
created envy and jealousy in other kingdoms. It was often

attacked by neighboring peoples, mainly raided by Malinke warriors who lived further south. These multiple attacks were not really a great concern for King Nedega as he had skilled and dedicated soldiers who fiercely defended the kingdom. Thus, they managed to win battles again and again. The king effectively ensured the peace, security, and prosperity of his people.

Indeed, during the reign of Nedega, the Kingdom of Dagomba expanded and became an economic power. The greatest strength of the kingdom was its legendary cavalry. At the head of this army was none other than the king's daughter, Princess Yennenga, a skilled warrior and a true horsewoman who conquered territories with her father's blessing.

Although Nedega ruled Dagomba with great authority, he was also considered to be a peace-loving king who was close to his people. He listened to problems and concerns, seeking input before making any decision that would affect the kingdom. Nedega was aware that, in the long run, a culture of fear would not make him a good leader, but an adversary.

He was seen as a wise and fair king who was as brilliant in diplomacy as he was in war. Sometimes he was able to avoid conflicts by skillful negotiation, while prioritizing the peace and prosperity of his kingdom.

During his reign, Nedega distinguished himself from other leaders with his visionary character and his principles of democratic monarchy and tolerance. Ahead of his time, he paved the way for the emancipation of women—an act of strength that made him a model African king.

Chapter 2

Tipgo, Whose Real Name Is Kayure

We all have an innate gift; it is up to us to discover it, to develop it, and to put it at the service of humanity.

—Anita Kane

Kayure, also known as Tipgo, was born in the middle of the dry season. The day of her birth was engraved in the memory of the elders of the Kingdom of Gambaga.

While Kayure's mother was in labor, the sky suddenly darkened. There was no rain, but the thunder rumbled so loudly that it drowned out the mother's cries of pain. The people of the kingdom had mixed reactions; some perceived this as a bad omen because there had been no rain.

Kayure's mother had successively lost four babies from unknown causes. This fifth child was born after this painful series of deaths. Needless to say, there was some fear that Kayure too might not survive. To make matters worse, this strange sign of nature during Kayure's birth left the whole kingdom perplexed as to her future.

It was decided that in order to ward off bad luck, the newborn child should be given a derisive name; this would symbolically reduce her to an uninteresting, almost-invisible thing. The idea was to deceive the evil forces responsible for the previous deaths by devaluing the baby. This naming ruse was traditionally used to preserve a child from the fate of infant mortality. Thus, the newborn was named Kayure, which means "nameless."

Kayure grew up happily, surrounded by the love of her parents. At that time, her father, Tiraogo, whose name means "male tree," was the kingdom's traditional healer; he treated and cured the sick using roots, leaves, bark, and herbs that he gathered in the bush or in the sacred forest. From a young age, Kayure loved to accompany her father on this gathering activity, and she enjoyed helping him concoct remedies and care for the sick.

Sometimes, when the sick came to consult Tiraogo, Kayure would imitate her father with all her seriousness and repeat his words that good health was the result of a harmony between the mind, the body, and the soul. According to this implacable logic, these patients had fallen ill because they had ignored the sacred and natural laws of wellness. This had the effect of bringing a laugh or a smile to the often-tense atmosphere.

As time went by, Tiraogo was amazed to see that Kayure had also inherited the gift of healing. Tiraogo himself had inherited it from his father. Thus, Tiraogo did not really have to teach Kayure much because his daughter had an innate gift for recognizing medicinal plants, and she did so with passion. Kayure seemed to communicate directly with nature. She would sometimes candidly say that she had secret friends who protected and guided her, but she seemed to be the only one who saw them.

At the age of seven, Kayure already understood that everything in nature had a soul and therefore breathed and deserved respect. Kayure was very skilled; with her small hands she was able to pick the young leaves of tiny plants, while preserving the roots so that they would come to life and continue to grow. Kayure impressed her father with the delicate way she put the soil back around the plant, with compassion and respect, as if she was saying a prayer.

Soon, Tiraogo realized that his daughter had more than just a gift for healing. Despite her young age, Kayure had premonitory dreams that surprised people because of their accuracy and precision. Even better, as a teenager, Kayure could sometimes heal her father's patients without the use of herbs or remedies. All she had to do was touch the patient in certain places on their body. Her hands seemed to emit a kind of healing and beneficial energy. She intuitively knew about the anatomy of the human body; it was a gift.

Thus, people began to whisper that Kayure was touched by the grace of the *kinkirsis* genies of the invisible world who symbolized the life forces and had supernatural powers.

Kinkirsis could be good or evil. However, Kayure seemed to be connected to the good genies. Her newfound healing powers earned her the nickname *Tipgo*, which means "care" or "treatment." This second name was adopted at the expense of her first, which was soon forgotten.

After her father went to join the ancestors, Tipgo naturally succeeded him to become the traditional healer of the kingdom and especially the royal court. It was known from her early childhood that Tipgo had this innate power of healing and that this gift had grown and become more refined as she had matured into an older woman. To express their gratitude after she performed a healing or solved a problem, the people of the kingdom would bring Tipgo all sorts of gifts, including sheep, roosters, guinea fowl, and sometimes gold or silver. When the people of the kingdom came to offer the gifts to Tipgo as an appreciation for saving a family member or themselves from certain death, Tipgo never failed to clarify that she was not the healer. She said that there was an unseen force in the healing that went beyond the herbs she prescribed. Her role as a healer was to support and facilitate the healing process; she was just an intermediary. Of course, this speech did not resonate because people saw only her and believed in only her.

Tipgo was not the only traditional healer in the kingdom. However, unlike the others and as suspected since her childhood, Tipgo had not only mastered the secret of medicinal plants, but she also had the ability to communicate with the ancestors, to contact the invisible world, and to know what was hidden. In the kingdom, she was considered the person who possessed true knowledge, who knew the principles of the universe, and who was blessed with clairvoyance, clairaudience, and wisdom. She knew the secrets of the sacred forest, the silence of the night, the rivers and the streams, the caves and the termite mounds. The people of the Kingdom of Dagomba had a respect intermingled with a certain fear for Tipgo.

Most people preferred to avoid Tipgo if they could. Usually, at the sight of her, children stopped playing, while the lively chattering of women would cease. However, because life often has its share of challenges which make human beings sometimes feel powerless, Tipgo's hut was rarely empty: the people of the kingdom went there to find peace of mind. They went to see Tipgo when they wanted answers to the great questions of life and when they were looking for supernatural support. The offerings recommended by Tipgo were religiously followed in order to ward off bad luck and obtain the approval of the ancestors.

When Tipgo was not busy interceding for someone or preparing a miraculous concoction for a sick person, she spent most of her time in silence, in nature. As she grew older, like many elderly women in the kingdom, one of her favorite pastimes was spinning cotton or sewing strips of cotton in front of her hut.

It should be noted that Tipgo's life journey hadn't always been so peaceful; she had suffered many storms. She experienced tragedies, including the loss of her only child and, a few months later, the disappearance of her husband into the forest who, despite extensive hunting, was never found. She hit rock bottom emotionally, physically, and socially. People had given her support and comfort as best they could, but nothing had helped: the pain and sadness persisted and stuck to her like a second skin.

However, one night Tipgo had a dream: it was a mysterious one that would give her life a new trajectory. She dreamed of being in the presence of her mother and father. It was as if she had become the little girl of yesteryear, all happy and carefree.

In this dream she was wearing a white dress made of cotton strips that she had woven herself. It was the very first garment she had made with her own hands. At the time, she felt great pride when she wore this dress and told anyone who would listen that it was the fruit of her labor. Indeed, as a little girl Tipgo had always been impressed to see how the women of the kingdom, especially her mother, grew cotton, harvested it, ginned it, and spun it into yarn for making clothes.

In her dream, Tipgo's parents held her by the hand in a place she did not recognize, but it was a very nice place. There were many trees and plants of all kinds with a variety of colors. The dream was so lucid that she could smell the pleasant scent of some of the medicinal plants that her father used. Her parents did not say a word to her, although she seemed to be able to communicate with them just by thoughts. Tipgo felt good and calm—a bit like a woman who has just given birth.

Suddenly, she was attracted by a rustling sound and turned her head toward the noise. She saw an elderly lady who was busy gathering leaves. The lady was singing and did not seem to be aware of the presence of other people. After picking some leaves, the lady put them in a small earthenware container and began to knead them. She extracted a greenish liquid which she used to coat her body. Even from a distance, Tipgo could feel that the lady radiated a soft and comforting energy.

Looking closer, Tipgo realized that this lady was in fact herself, and she had a bright glow and serenity on her face.

Without understanding how, she found herself in her hut where she saw herself slumped with a haggard look on her mat, almost devoid of life. Later, she saw a lady arrive whom she did not know or recognize. The good lady had come to care for her because Tipgo seemed unable to do anything. The unknown lady helped her to wash and dress. She wanted to ask her parents what all this meant, and then she realized that they were no longer there. She found herself alone with unanswered questions.

Tipgo woke up with a start and in a sweat. She was upset, and she knew that it was more than a simple dream because the deceased who return from the hereafter are bearers of messages. It was already dawn; the kingdom would soon come alive. She managed to drag herself outside and sat down right at the entrance to her hut. The cool morning air did her a world of good. She replayed the dream in her mind, trying to unravel every little detail. She was shocked by the contrast between the two different Tipgos in the dream. It was like night and day. She spent several days meditating on the meaning and significance of what she had experienced in the dream.

Eventually, Tipgo realized that if she continued to react negatively to her unpleasant situation it could lead to a greater disaster. She understood that in her current state there were two options available to her: choose to remain in this almost vegetative and painful state for the rest of her life or choose to recover, knowing that she had the ability to do so within herself. With everything that happened to her, she could either feel sorry for herself or consider what happened to her as a gift and use it.

However, it was up to her and her alone to make the decision. That is the law of freewill.

A few days after her strange dream, despite her condition,

Tipgo asked to be taken to the sacred forest. She wanted the leaves of a shrub that could only be found in that forest. In retrospect, she knew that her healing would come through these leaves, and she knew exactly what type of leaf because she had seen it in her dream.

The days that followed her visit to the sacred forest were pivotal. Tipgo went into a spiritual retreat. She did not speak to anyone for three days; she had explicitly asked not to have visitors, and the people of the kingdom respected her wish despite their concern as they wondered if this was the end for her.

On the morning of the fourth day, Tipgo found some peace; inwardly and symbolically, she thanked the pain, the sorrow, and the sadness for their presence, and she was grateful for this experience that she had lived. She decided to release them from her mind, to let them go because their mission was over: she had understood and made her choice.

Tipgo made the choice to go back up the slope and, from that moment on, her healing was dazzling and complete as if the evil that had been eating away at her for years had never existed. She vowed to spend the rest of her life relieving the pain of others in all its forms.

By then in her sixties, she made it her mission to spend the rest of her life entirely in the service of others. She was very compassionate and empathetic toward her fellow human beings, and she understood that as humans we all have intrinsic value and share similar aspirations, fears, and struggles. She tried to as best she could to help alleviate the physical and emotional suffering of others and did so with passion and dedication. She understood that this was the purpose of her life on this Earth, and she needed to know this suffering herself in order to understand it in others. This experience had been painful but necessary for her to evolve and reach her full potential. Indeed, Tipgo understood with time that there had been no mistake: life always brings us the experiences and trials that will be the most useful for our evolution, and she was the living proof of this.

Tipgo clearly understood that the most difficult moments can be our best teachers; it is not what happens to us that decides our fates, but rather our reaction to what happens to us. And if we have the wisdom and courage to change the way we look at things, the things we look at also change.

Sometimes it takes years before we can look back and say we are glad something adverse happened; Tipgo was able to say that in hindsight because she saw how it made her stronger and wiser. From her experience, Tipgo encouraged her patients to remember that when we lose something that we deeply appreciate, that experience opens the door to something much better, but we must be willing to see it and receive it.

Chapter 3

The Gift of Intuition

We know the truth not only through our reason
but also through our heart.

—Blaise Pascal, *Pensées*

Despite having many wives, King Nedega was unable to have
children, and he suffered in silence. This was a difficult and
embarrassing situation for the royal family.

Was it the king himself who had a problem? Was it his
wives, or was it just a whim of fate? It was hard to say, but after
many years of prayers and sacrifices to the ancestors, Nedega
finally had a daughter; however, he had been hoping for a son
to ensure the continuation of his reign.

The Kingdom of Gambaga was patriarchal: women were
not allowed to reign. Succession to the throne was by order
of male primogeniture. This means that the eldest legitimate
son of the king has priority for succession to the throne. In

such a context, having a male heir ensures the lineage and the perpetuity of the family's reign.

Nedega therefore wished more than anything else to have a son to be certain that his lineage would continue to reign. In the event that King Nedega did not have a son to succeed him, the first in the order of succession would be a close male relative, such as a brother or cousin.

In that case, the council of elders of the kingdom would decide by agreement who would be the heir to the throne because to claim the throne it was not enough to have direct blood ties with the king. It was also important to have the qualities of a good leader.

The first child of the king was Princess Yennenga. Historical accounts do not report whether Yennenga's arrival brought good luck to the king by opening the way for a line of other children. Yennenga was the only child of the king with Queen Napoko. Having a son would have satisfied the king's ego. However, at the sight of his daughter, who resembled him as closely as the resemblance between two drops of water, Nedega was very moved and quickly forgot his disappointment of not having a male heir to the throne.

When the child was born, the royal drum announced the news and was immediately echoed by the other drums. Soon, from the smallest to the largest neighboring kingdoms, everyone knew that King Nedega had a daughter. Without really saying it out loud, many subjects of the king thought it was time.

The royal family prepared for the ceremony to welcome the

baby into the world. This was an opportunity to announce the child's name and its significance. In the Kingdom of Dagomba, no name was given at random. There was always a meaning, a story, or an intention associated with each name. Names could be taken from another person's name, given in reference to a birth circumstance, or related to unseen beings.

The princess was named *Poko*, which means "woman." However, she was later nicknamed *Yennenga*, which means "slender" because of her slender build. The king celebrated with a generous feast in Gambaga. For several days the village was alive with the sound of drums and balafons, and the millet beer flowed endlessly. The chiefs of the neighboring kingdoms sent emissaries to congratulate Nedega and to bring gifts. The gifts, ranging from refined shea butter to gold jewelry, came from all over and cluttered the hut of Napoko, the new queen mother.

The women of the kingdom adorned themselves with their most beautiful jewelry and competed to see who could wear the most beautiful woven cotton loincloth. This was the ideal occasion to show off one's prosperity and to dazzle one's neighbors. The griots sang the praises of the king, his father, and his father's father.

As the years went by, Yennenga grew up well and was admired by her father for her sweetness and infectious energy. The king adored her and cherished her with all his heart.

From her earliest childhood, the princess showed a great passion for animals. She loved to play with the little sheep and goats in the hut and to watch the birth of animals; she was not even afraid to see small wild animals wandering around the royal concession. Injured animals or orphaned chicks were brought to her. Her passion for animals was known throughout the kingdom. With the help of Tipgo, the traditional herbalist who knew the secrets of plants and whom Yennenga affectionately called "grandmother," she concocted wonderful traditional cures for sick animals. The princess was a quick learner and had infinite patience when it came to applying concoctions to wounds or feeding abandoned small animals.

Of all the animals, Yennenga preferred horses. A horse would spend hours galloping in the bush but would never fail to return to humans—this fascinated her enormously. She watched with wonder these beasts that shone with beauty, strength, instinct, and intelligence. They seemed able to read her innermost being.

Like all young girls and boys growing up, Yennenga had dreams. One of those dreams was simply to ride a horse. However, this was a big problem, because in the tradition of her people the horse was reserved for men only. Society was very much defined by gender—women had very different roles than men. A woman's role was related to family concerns such as taking care of the children and the home. A man was considered the head of the family and had the sole decision-making power. A woman owed a man respect and obedience. As a result, men and women were not considered equal.

But Yennenga had a stubborn temperament. Although she was aware of the status of women in the kingdom, she stubbornly refused to obey the ban on riding horses. Knowing that her father almost never refused her anything, she decided to try her luck and asked him for permission to ride one of his beasts. The king was hesitant at first, but after several insistent requests from Yennenga, he began to seriously consider the idea.

In his heart, Nedega knew that Yennenga was not a child like others. He saw in the princess a girl who had intrinsic abilities beyond the ordinary and who carried within her a world of possibilities. Still, how could a girl be allowed to do something that had previously been the preserve of men? It would be against the traditions of his ancestors. As king, he was the main guarantor of the traditions, along with the elders around him.

Thus, the king faced a dilemma: he was divided between following tradition or following his heart. Yet, he was very comfortable with the idea of letting the princess ride. He knew it would be good for the kingdom, but he didn't know why or how. He could hear a little voice inside, like an unconscious reasoning, that urged him to act in that direction. He couldn't explain it logically to the elders of the kingdom, but he knew it was the right thing to do.

Despite what the king knew intuitively, the decision was not taken lightly. Nedega was a great scholar of the ancestral traditions and was knowledgeable enough to know that the ancestors had to be consulted in such decisions lest he provoke their anger.

Nedega called on old Tipgo and explained Yennenga's request and his thoughts. Tipgo agreed that such a step would require agreement with the will of the ancestors. She promised to do what was necessary and to return to him with an answer, whether positive or negative.

After several days of rituals and sleepless nights, old Tipgo finally requested an audience with the king. That day, she got up earlier than usual, washed her face and cleaned her teeth before performing some incantations. She went to the sacred forest before the first light of dawn. The whole kingdom was still asleep, and her journey to the forest was very quick.

In the sacred forest, the trees seemed to be arranged in a very specific order. There were thick, sometimes-thorny bushes followed by tall trees. Some had a tangle of vines around their trunks that reached all the way to the top; others with dense, colorful foliage seemed to welcome visitors. This was not an arrangement made by the hand of a human being, but by God himself.

Old Tipgo stopped near the largest tree in the middle of the sacred forest. Nothing moved. Only the rustling of foliage interrupted the silence from time to time. Was it the wind and the rustling of the birds' wings or the breath of the ancestors? It was hard to say.

Old Tipgo knelt. The ground was a little wet from the morning dew, but the sexagenarian was too preoccupied to notice. She wasn't usually careless. However, all night long she had been tossing and turning on her mat, unable to sleep. Before addressing the king, she wanted to confirm what she had seen in her dream that night.

After her morning trek through the sacred forest, old Tipgo

went straight to the palace. After the customary greetings, she cleared her throat and addressed the king:

"The ancestors have spoken. May your will be in accord with theirs. Here, I am a guide, and my duty is to pass on the message to you. The ancestors are favorable with the idea of letting the princess ride. However, sacrifices must be made to ask for their protection and to thank them for their cooperation," said Tipgo.

One of the dogs in the court began to bark frantically, and old Tipgo stopped talking. Everyone knew that dogs do not bark without cause. When the dog barked, it was because it had seen something: a stranger, an animal, or one of those beings invisible to humans. After a moment of silence, the old woman scratched her back, gave a smile that showed gums lined with a few teeth, and continued:

"According to the ancestors, it will be rather beneficial to the kingdom if the princess rides a horse, but we must also remember that every action has a consequence. Sometimes the deeper meaning can escape us humans if we don't take the long view. The storms that pass by and disturb our peace of mind also light our way if we take care to know their deeper meaning. Thus, each trial of life should be seen as a teaching and not as an enemy. The most important thing is to remember them and understand their true meaning."

Old Tipgo had spoken slowly and softly, weighing each word as if she wanted to be sure that the deeper meaning did not escape the king. She took her snuffbox, which she always carried with her, and opened it, dipped her index finger in it, and put the brown powder on her tongue. She gently closed the box while scanning the horizon with an incisive look and her forehead wrinkled, which had the effect of making the atmosphere even more mystical.

Nedega knew the sexagenarian well and could see that she looked more mysterious than usual, but he couldn't put his finger on the reason for this mystery. Nor could he understand why Tipgo would make a long speech to answer a simple question.

Tipgo had confirmed to the king what he already sensed and knew in his heart. Although the answer of the clairvoyant was not a surprise, he still felt a certain discomfort, like a lump in his throat, at the end of their conversation. There was still that little voice inside that told him that there was more to know and that old Tipgo had not told him everything.

This strange feeling persisted for several days and grew like a whisper when the king was in moments of solitude. His uneasiness was so deep that he decided to confide in Napoko.

"*M'ba sida*, you are very worried," said Napoko in a reassuring tone.

"M'ba sida" meant "my dear husband," and this was the affectionate and respectful name the queen used when addressing her husband. Often Napoko addressed the king as "Yennenga's father." As a wife, she was required to address her husband in the polite manner and would never call Nedega directly by his name.

"If there is a threat of any danger to the kingdom," she

continued, "Tipgo will not fail to inform you. This bad feeling you have is probably the result of fatigue due to your heavy responsibilities as king."

After thinking about it for a long time, Nedega called Tipgo again in the presence of the notables of the kingdom and asked her if there was anything else he should know. Unperturbed, old Tipgo sat on the mat with her hands in her lap, looking away.

"I have given you the information you need to decide, King Nedega. It would be inappropriate to ask the ancestors the same question again when they have already answered it," said Tipgo.

Addressing the notables present, she added, "Remember that life is a journey in which we learn lessons and receive information through our various experiences at the right time. I say to you again, there is no harm in honoring Yennenga's request."

In the days that followed, the queen noticed that old Tipgo seemed to have grown closer to the princess, but she did not find this alarming or strange. She put it down to the effect of loneliness and the weight of old age.

After a few more days of reflection, the king decided to ignore the internal murmuring and concentrate on more concrete and pressing matters.

To begin with, Yennenga rode horses of her choice in the royal court. She liked to be on their backs and feel the movement of their bodies. She liked this privileged contact which had redoubled her passion for horses—a passion she shared with the king, her father. Later, she accompanied her father on his long rides. She quickly became a formidable and extraordinary horsewoman.

Of course, this non-traditional freedom given to the princess was not to everyone's taste. Some people in the kingdom were offended, and there were whispers that the chief was wrong to give his daughter so much freedom. Moreover, breaking these prohibitions could have serious consequences for the kingdom. However, Nedega, with a mischievous smile, replied that there was no harm in a girl riding a horse, especially since, according to Tipgo, the ancestors had authorized it. Moreover, had he not offered sacrifices to the ancestors to thank them and ask for their protection?

In time, Yennenga proved to be a skilled rider. She could ride better than some of the king's warriors. She took a liking to one horse in particular: a white stallion.

Chapter 4

Little Yennenga Becomes a Young Woman

The child who is from a young age accustomed
to watering learns to water.

—*Arabian Proverb*

Like all other girls in her age-group, Yennenga received the education traditionally reserved for young females. This education would make her a successful wife and devoted mother. According to the tradition of the kingdom, the transition from girlhood to maidenhood was a process that could last several years and started when the girl was between twelve and fourteen years old. Thus, Yennenga's apprenticeship was gradual; she gradually abandoned her childlike status and adopted the attitude and tasks of a young woman, which included fetching water, carrying heavy bundles of wood, pounding and grinding millet, preparing meals, and maintaining the house. She also learned the techniques for preparing millet beer and performing agricultural work. Of all the training, the preparation of meals was a most significant task because it was associated not only with the woman's function as a provider, but also with sexuality. Indeed, in a polygamous union, it was the norm for the wife who prepared the meal to spend the night with the husband.

It was only after passing this formative stage that Yennenga and her companions were considered fully-fledged young women. Napoko, Yennenga's mother, was primarily responsible for her daughter's education, both in terms of teaching feminine techniques and the obligations of future wives. In the kingdom, the educational role of mothers also extended to the control of their daughters' outings and flirtations with young men, which mothers had to suppress. The mother would thus be held responsible for the deviant behavior of her daughter.

However, as the saying goes, "It takes a whole village to raise a child." Queen Napoko, like all the other mothers of the kingdom, was not alone in this responsibility. The elders also participated in the training of their younger sisters as wives and mothers devoted to the marital family. These training rites were central to the younger sisters' relationship with the older generation. Despite this hierarchy, this relationship was marked by humor, teasing, and affection.

Yennenga's training lasted just over a year. After this training, the young princess enjoyed a little more freedom in that she was allowed to take care of herself in terms of choice of adornments, body care, coquetry, and even banter with young men. Some of her companions could also engage in personal economic activities, such as making food or millet beer to sell but, due to her status as princess, Yennenga was restricted from some of these activities.

She was leaving the world of childhood behind and entering the clan of young women. The king and queen were proud of their daughter.

Shortly after this period of training and initiation, Yennenga was quickly taken in hand by the king, who saw in her the eldest son he had never had. Of course, Nedega had several wives and perhaps other descendants—we don't really know. But, as the eldest, Yennenga was the child he loved the most. The king loved Yennenga for several reasons. First, she was the fruit of his union with his favorite, Napoko. In addition, she resembled him in many ways: her looks—her eyes, her chin, and sometimes her unconscious tics; and her wholesome and lively character—her intelligence, her determination and, most of all, her sense of justice.

The princess grew up in contact with warriors. She accompanied her father on hunting trips and even learned to use traditional weapons. Little by little, she became an expert in the use of weapons: she used the assegai, the javelin, the spear, and the bow to perfection. She was not afraid of falls from her horse because she knew how to cushion them. The risk of falling was an integral part of training. Yennenga had mastered the proper technique to fall safely. Her strong, muscular legs encircled her mount, allowing her to stay on the animal's back for a long time. The princess loved to ride alone because she loved the feeling of freedom and symbiosis with the animal. She enjoyed this feeling of power—a feeling forbidden for women according to the traditional female education.

Yennenga was therefore granted the right to accompany her father on the battlefields. In time, she began to lead the cavalry. She helped her father protect the kingdom from recurring attacks by other tribes and thus became the army's indispensable warlord. The intrepid princess led the military operations with authority, but few outside the kingdom knew that this fiery warlord was a woman because she wore no feminine finery, and nothing distinguished her from her fellow fighters in battle.

It was a discovery to all that a woman could have this talent, which had previously only been possessed by men. However, this discovery upset the order of things. Although the warriors did not say it aloud, the princess was admired by all. The princess was highly respected, and her orders were followed as scrupulously as if she were the king himself.

Thus, the ancestors seemed to have been right to allow the king to grant his daughter this freedom.

Chapter 5

Greatness Does Not Rhyme with Perfection

The gem cannot be polished without friction,
nor man perfected without trials.

- Chinese Proverb

Although Yennenga led the royal cavalry, she was not a "tomboy." One look at her was enough to immediately fall under her spell. Sure, she had muscle, but she also had enough grace and femininity to attract romantic attention. She had ebony skin and a feline gait, while being tall and slender—she lived up to her nickname of Yennenga: the slender girl. Moreover, she had a beautiful face with fine, harmonious, and majestic features. She exuded a beautiful mix of femininity and masculinity—an unusual combination in this very gendered society—which gave her an undeniable charisma. Her father's fame also made her a desirable ally. There was no shortage of opportunities for marriage.

King Nedega was wildly proud of his daughter—perhaps a little too proud. He would tell the elders of the kingdom about her prowess in the battlefield and how she could wield weapons with ease and agility. Sometimes he would call her before the elders to give a demonstration because a picture was worth a thousand words.

Thus, Yennenga was like a jewel that he took pleasure in showing off at the great royal festivals. Although the most important families of the kingdom dreamed of marrying their son to the beautiful princess, the king delayed marriage. He had no thoughts of marrying her; he even seemed to forget that she was a woman! His ambition for the moment was to make her a great warrior in command of his army.

As tradition dictated, marriage was a discussion for the men. Therefore, only the men had the privilege of choosing the one who would marry their daughter. This rule also applied to the royal court. Queen Napoko suffered greatly because of this; as a mother she wanted her daughter to marry and have children of her own. Her hands were tied, because marriage and a royal lineage did not seem to be Nedega's plan for Yennenga at that moment.

Surprisingly, even though the young princess was motivated by her military prowess, she did not only think about this: she had other ambitions and dreamed of another life, like the one her friends of the same generation were leading. All the girls her age were at least engaged, and some were married. Some were already nursing their first child, while she, Yennenga, spent most of her time wielding weapons and on the battlefields.

While Nedega never refused his princess anything, when it came to marriage he insisted that it was a very serious decision that should not be taken lightly. He said he was willing to wait for the opportune time because he needed the best son-in-law for his daughter.

The suitors followed one after the other. There were young men who pleased the princess and she dreamed of becoming their wife. But, at each request for marriage, her father was categorically opposed. None of them was good enough for his daughter. He made excuses to justify his refusal to the families of these suitors.

Yennenga tried several times to talk to him, but she could not establish a fruitful dialogue. Each time she raised the question, the king would reply sharply that there was no hurry.

The truth was that the princess's charisma, great skill, and bravery on the battlefield proved to the king that he had an heiress worthy of taking over the kingdom. However, if he married off his daughter, whether her husband was of royal blood or not, he would lose Yennenga because of her status as a woman, because she would become part of her husband's family. He consciously decided that Yennenga was too precious to his people and should not be married—at least not for the time being.

His intentions were less clear to some people, but obvious

to others. Criticism was rife in the kingdom. In the market, under the trees, there were whispers, discussions, agitation, and passionate debate.

During his reign, Nedega had earned the respect of his people and was seen as a hero. Now, however, the people were divided on the subject.

First, there were those who were obsessed with the idea that a hero should be perfect: they had clothed their king in the mantle of perfection, and now they had every reason to be disappointed. In their minds, Nedega's attitude toward his daughter's marriage nullified all his good parenting qualities and all the many extraordinary things he had done. Yes, once Nedega had a good heart, listened to his people, and defended the kingdom at the risk of his own life. Now, he was called a tyrannical king who controlled his daughter and took advantage of her extraordinary qualities to maintain the reputation of his powerful army and ensure the security of the kingdom. He was no longer the perfect hero they thought he was; this was a painful and difficult reality to accept. They had accepted, or rather tolerated, the king permitting the young princess to ride animals. Obviously, this non-traditional freedom granted to the princess was not to everyone's liking, especially because it allowed other young girls of the kingdom to dream of unattainable goals and could open the way to libertinage and revolt. A girl must marry, have children, and take care of her husband.

On the other hand, there were those who accepted that the king was a man of value who defended what he believed in, but who also had his weaknesses and faults like any human being. They maintained that Nedega had a great capacity to respond to difficulties, to anticipate, to correct, and even to adapt if necessary. For this group, mistakes did not negate the value of the effort made.

There were certainly some decisions that Nedega had not made correctly, but he had done his best and acted in the interests of the kingdom. For these people, Nedega was a great king and would remain so, even if he seemed to fall from glory.

Between these two groups there were the undecided and the neutral who, for various reasons, preferred not to have an opinion.

Nedega was well aware that he was the object of criticism: some was compassionate; some, spiteful gossip. After all, what leader was not? But he was able to step back from all the excitement. He was aware that all this was part of the responsibilities of a king. Early in his childhood, he had learned not to take what others said or did to him personally. Indeed, he understood that each person saw the world in a unique way through his or her own eyes, colored by expectations, emotions, and beliefs about what is right or wrong, just or unjust.

As a king, Nedega was prepared for moments like this, when he would face potentially hurtful criticism. Far from losing sight of the legitimate sensitivities of his people and the need to maintain their trust, he was still determined to follow his heart and fulfill his responsibilities as king regarding the future of the kingdom. After all, he was still in very good health. The inheritance of the throne could wait a little longer.

Chapter 6

A Dream Without Action Remains a Dream

The only limit to the height of your achievements is the reach of your dreams and your willingness to work hard for them.

—Michelle Obama

The king's constant refusals began to seriously hurt the princess. Yennenga was upset; for the first time in her life, she could not establish a real dialogue with her father. She had lost her beautiful smile and enthusiasm, ate little, and spent long nights thinking. She was entering her twenties and, all of a sudden, life seemed complicated and bland. She wondered all day long how she was going to make her dream of getting married come true. The sight of her friends breastfeeding their children haunted her mind relentlessly. She too wanted to experience the love and joy of motherhood.

Yennenga felt she was getting older, so she knew she had to do something. She didn't think that waiting patiently for a miracle to happen and for the king to suddenly change his mind was the best approach. She had to find a way to make her father see reason. For that, she needed a sympathetic ear to listen and guide her. She was quite close to elderly Tipgo, but she had never dared to talk to her about her desire to marry for fear that the clairvoyant would predict that her dream would never come true.

Tipgo was a very optimistic person by nature, but she was also realistic. Yennenga spent a lot of time with Tipgo and benefited from her teachings and advice. Tipgo had opened her mind to the mysteries of life. Yennenga knew more than anyone that we should not underestimate the power of what we believe on our ability to accomplish an action, because everything starts with thought. She was determined to hold on to any glimmer of hope, even if it meant avoiding confiding in Grandma Tipgo, whom she loved with all her heart.

Yet, one day, while helping Grandma Tipgo prepare a remedy for a horse with a leg injury, the traditional healer began to speak, as if she read Yennenga's mind.

"We all have dreams in our lives that we would like to fulfill. However, the dream that keeps you awake at night or makes you get up early in the morning, the dream that creates such a tension in you that just thinking about it makes you exalt with joy—that dream is worth fighting for. You can't afford to live with the regret of not having tried even once to achieve it. There is no worse suffering than living your life with regrets."

Then, with a firm and mysterious tone that implied she was imparting a secret wisdom, Tipgo revealed this to Yennenga:

"Never let your fear of acting be greater than your dream. When you are dominated by fear, you are no longer a free person. Trust your intuition and the light beings that guide you, and you will not be disappointed. The truth is that the veil between the visible and invisible worlds is thin, but those who open themselves to the possibility can feel it and have access to it."

After a long pause, Tipgo added, "Even if it is still difficult to perceive, keep in mind that the trials you are going through now will serve you in the future because they prepare you for something greater. One day, which is still a little distant, you will make a long journey alone on horseback; if you let the horse guide you on the direction to take, you will arrive at your destination."

Yennenga did not understand what she meant, but as Tipgo said this, she looked at Yennenga with a piercing gaze, as if she wanted to impregnate her whole being with every word she had just said. Her gaze was so intense that Yennenga felt a shiver run down her spine.

Tipgo continued in a softer tone. "It is normal and even useful sometimes to feel fear in dangerous situations because fear is meant to protect us by keeping us alert and ready to act. However, when that fear becomes irrational and paralyzing, we must not let it overwhelm us. You are bold when you find yourself leading an army or on a battlefield. But you must also learn to overcome your fear in order to be in charge of your own life, Yennenga. You have the ability to control that fear and, if you can control it, you will strengthen your ability to act and at the same time open the door to a multitude of possibilities. Courageous people act despite their fear."

Even though Yennenga was quite close to Tipgo, the princess found her to be a bit strange at times. Yet, she also knew that underneath her mystical shell, the old lady had a heart full of compassion, love, and kindness.

Yennenga had great respect and love for Grandma Tipgo. She listened dutifully when she told her stories of the past or when she taught her the secrets of plants and shared with her meaningful life experiences. In good times and in bad, Tipgo always had appropriate sacred formulas that she recited, and Yennenga had memorized some of these. She loved these words of wisdom and the comforting effect that came from repeating them over and over again; for her, it was direct evidence of the power of the spoken word.

She had also learned from Tipgo to read nature's signs. This was the case when Yennenga noticed that some of the trees at the entrance to the forest were being over-grazed by animals; she expressed her concern to Tipgo. With a smile, Tipgo told her that nature could take care of itself. She explained that, with time, these trees would increase their production of tannin to be inedible, but the most extraordinary thing was that these trees were able to communicate to other trees located miles away to do the same. Yennenga was both amazed and mystified by this discovery.

She would never contradict Grandma! Their relationship was based on respect for age, experience, and wisdom.

Yennenga finally decided to ask her mother, the queen, for her advice. As a girl, Yennenga slept with her mother in the same hut. While boys left the female sphere around the age of seven, girls were required to reside in their mother's hut until they married. Yennenga was therefore under her mother's authority. As a daughter, it was only the marriage act that allowed her to leave the parental court, to relinquish her paternal guardianship and take on that of her husband.

Thus, a mother would be held responsible for her daughter's deviant attitude, whether it was an accusation of laziness, libertinism, or rebellion against an arranged marriage. If a daughter of the kingdom was to refuse a husband or a marriage, this could expose her mother to repudiation, which was the ultimate sanction. Thus, the destiny of mothers and daughters was strongly intertwined.

Yennenga prepared herself mentally to have this conversation with her mother; although she was close to the queen, she was still shy about discussing certain subjects. When evening came, she went to find her mother in her hut where she retired at nightfall. Yennenga knew that Napoko was suffering as much as she was from the king's attitude, but her status as a woman did not give her much power.

Yennenga opened up to her mother in a simple and sincere way. She spoke of her dreams, of the kind of husband she would like, of the number of children she would like to have. She let her mother know that she felt ready for marriage and referred to her peers who were expecting their second child. She spoke of the sorrow she felt regarding the king's unusual attitude, though she did not blame him. Yennenga spoke in a monologue.

Despite her silence, Napoko listened to her daughter with great interest; she admired the sincerity of her account. She thought her daughter had some unusual ideas, such as the audacity to dare to hope that she could choose her husband; but she did not dwell on this aspect, which she thought was a conversation they could have later on. For now, her daughter needed her support and love. She just wanted to be listened to, to be understood and supported.

As a child, Napoko had never dared to have such dreams. She had not chosen her husband; she had simply obeyed her father's orders. She knew very little about her husband before the wedding, but with time she got to know him better and even loved him; and the king returned her love well. She couldn't complain; until now Nedega had been a good husband for her and was also a good king for the kingdom. She herself did not understand the king's intentions for Yennenga. The king seemed to have lost his mind. Napoko's pain was twofold because she suffered from the fact that her daughter was still single, and she had to endure the innuendos and mockery of the other women in the royal court. Napoko's pain was silent, but it was very painful. She tried to hide it as best she could when she spoke to Yennenga.

Her mother advised her to get her father's attention by planting a field of okra, which she was to let ripen and rot without picking. This way of addressing the king was borderline extreme, but Yennenga was willing to accept the consequences of her actions and decisions. What was the worst that could happen? Whatever it was, she was willing to accept the consequences.

So, following her mother's advice, Yennenga found a piece of land not far from the palace where she grew a field of okra. Later, the vegetable plants grew well, and Yennenga let them ripen, then let them wither and rot without picking them.

One day, on his morning walk, Nedega saw the wilted okra field. First intrigued, then outraged and indignant because of the state of the field, he returned to the court.

"Who sowed okra and then let it wither and rot without harvesting it?"

"We don't own this field. Why don't you go and ask your daughter Yennenga?" said one of the women with a touch of irony in her voice.

For Nedega, Yennenga was the perfect child in every sense. For once, there was an opportunity to reproach this perfect child; this did not displease some of the women of the royal court, who barely concealed their jealousy of the preferential treatment that Yennenga and Queen Napoko enjoyed.

The king called Yennenga and asked her the reason for this neglect. As her mother had told her, she answered, "Father, you are perfectly right. As you know, okra must be picked fresh. But these vegetables are drying on the plant. In the same way, you are letting me wither as this field of okra withers. If a ripe vegetable is not picked in time, it either hardens or rots on the tree."

Within the kingdom, it was well known that okra was a condiment that connoted the female body. When it withered, it became rough, to the point of having spines that made it unfit for consumption.

The king felt a ball of emotion rise inside him. He was furious, but he did not let it show. The princess's reply bordered on insolence, but the king pretended not to understand. He remained thoughtful for some time, and with a calm and measured gesture he told his daughter that she could leave.

Perplexed, Yennenga did not know what to think. What did this silence mean? She knew that her father rarely spoke without deliberating his thoughts and choosing his words carefully. He did not mix his words with his emotions. As he said, emotions could change, but words could not; the king knew the power of words. He knew that words were not just a series of sounds. Spoken words had energy and power—a powerful force that was the privilege of humans. This force could be used constructively, such as to encourage, help, bless, and heal; or destructively, such as to hurt, curse, humiliate, insult, or belittle. It is well known that a forked tongue hurts more than a tripping foot.

Thus, when faced with conflicting situations where there was a risk of inappropriate use of words, the king would only smile or remain silent.

Yennenga secretly hoped that her father would soon return with an answer. She waited in vain for a sign from him or a word from her mother. But every time she was in Nedega's presence, he spoke to her about things that had absolutely nothing to do with her current concerns, and Yennenga cried internally. She had imagined all sorts of consequences to her action, but she had never thought of a long and heavy silence. For her, indifference was the worst torture.

Days, weeks, months passed, but the king remained silent about the story of the okra field, as if the incident had never happened. Yennenga was shaken; nothing seemed to overcome Nedega's determination not to give in to her desire to marry. Given her education, Yennenga knew that another confrontation with the king on this subject would be highly inappropriate. Even her mother Napoko would not have supported her in this. She had made her message clear, and it was up to the king to come back to her if he wanted to; no one could force the king. For Yennenga, this was a double instruction because the king was her father, and this rule also governed the daughter–father relationships in the whole kingdom.

Chapter 7

The Courage to Choose

I learned that courage was not the absence of
fear, but the triumph over it. The brave man
is not he who does not feel afraid, but he who
conquers that fear.

—Nelson Mandela, *Long Walk to Freedom*

Tired of the war with her father, Yennenga made the wise
decision not to confront him again because she knew her limit;
"Eggs do not dance with stones," they say.

She understood Nedega's dreams, but they were not her
own, and she refused to endorse them. She loved her father
and her kingdom, but she did not see herself as his successor.
She was torn by her desires as a woman, but these desires were
incompatible with her status as the head of the army.

So, the princess began to entertain the idea of leaving the
Kingdom of Dagomba. She finally convinced herself that
leaving was the right thing to do; trying to impose herself

would be a waste of time and energy. However, the idea of leaving also brought a flood of worries. Where could she go without the powerful royal army finding her in record time? She also knew that none of the neighboring kingdoms would agree to give asylum to the daughter of the great King Nedega for fear of reprisals.

Despite these concerns, she also believed that life had more to offer her. She did not know if she would ever experience the joy of being a wife and mother, but she was certain that she was not destined to rule.

Grandmother Tipgo had taught her that the intention behind every action is a fundamental principle that governs every moment of life. The elderly never did anything without a clear intention, and Tipgo strongly recommended that Yennenga follow this example. Several times, Tipgo had reminded her to always determine her intention clearly before taking any action—even for something as simple as drinking water. This was especially important because the outcome of the action would be determined by the underlying intention, like a cause-and-effect relationship. To determine the true intention behind the action, Tipgo strongly suggested that she use the intelligence of her heart, not her head.

Thus, the search for and gathering of medicinal plants was always preceded by an intention, and one should not gather more than necessary. Tipgo had taught her the importance of living in harmony with the Earth that feeds us.

With her plan to escape in mind, Yennenga felt these words

of advice from Grandmother Tipgo reach deep within her. She mulled over the idea, and thought more with her heart than with her head. The message that came to her was that the real motivation behind her desire to leave Gambaga was not to escape her father and her beloved people, but to find meaning and purpose in her life, which seemed stagnant.

Tipgo had not only taught Yennenga the secret of medicinal plants. She had taken every opportunity in her company to teach her the principles and laws that governed the cosmos. In this way, Tipgo passed on her deep respect for all forms of life and urged her to always act in accordance with the principles of the universe. Sometimes, Yennenga didn't quite understand, but Grandma Tipgo would simply tell her that one day she would. What doesn't make sense now will make sense later on.

One evening, just after sunset, Koudbila, a lady of the royal court, came to see Queen Napoko to talk about Yennenga, whom she had found to be a little strange for some time. The princess's friends had also noticed that she was becoming distant and had discussed this at length among themselves. Because of her friendship with the queen, Koudbila felt it was her duty to inform her.

Indeed, since the incident of the okra field, Yennenga, who was usually very smiley and liked to joke with her friends, hardly said hello to them. She no longer frequented the places where the girls gathered. Napoko had an idea of why this was and did her best to reassure Yennenga.

"Don't be discouraged. Hang in there and hope. Your father

will eventually understand that marriage is better than war for a woman. Here, everything has an end, and there is a natural self-correction that rectifies what should not be. I only ask you to be a little more patient with your father."

Yennenga listened to her mother with interest. She saw and understood her helplessness in this situation. She was a woman, and marriage was a man's decision. The queen had no room for maneuver.

One moonless night, Yennenga was overcome with an irresistible urge to break free. She could no longer bear to stay in her "golden prison" in Gambaga. While the whole palace was in a deep sleep, animated by a courage that surprised even her, the princess put on her man's clothes that were also her warrior's clothes and, with extreme caution, she crept to the royal stable. She silently mounted her favorite horse, the white stallion.

The reckless rider rode into the bush and began a long journey into the unknown. She let herself be guided by the horse, which became her faithful companion throughout this flight and search for freedom.

Yennenga and her horse seemed to be alone in the world. It was dark. Nevertheless, the stars, as if in collusion, lit up a path with a faint glow through the leaves of the tall trees of the forest—just enough to allow her to see the passage.

After a few hours of galloping through the dark night, Yennenga had no idea where she was or where she was going. She was alone, completely alone, in the dark bush. All along the way, she could hear the cries of hungry beasts on the prowl, which made her heart race.

Grandma Tipgo's fearful stories about the mysteries of the night, genies, spirits, and the secrets of the forest came back to her mind. Despite her experience with long arduous journeys to the battlefields, she suddenly felt her warrior's courage leave her and fear invade her. Her stomach churned.

From experience, she knew that to counteract fear she had to control her thoughts. She also knew that she could deliberately choose what kind of thoughts she wanted to have. She began to replay in her mind, like a movie, the different challenges she had overcome so far. She remembered the first time she rode a horse, the different battles she had won, the admiring look on her father's face, and what Grandma Tipgo had told her about fear the first time she had been on a battlefield.

Tipgo had also taught her that when we are in a fearful situation, we can also lean on our powerful ancestors from within and without our family lineage to support and give us strength and confidence. We don't need to know all their names: we just have to call upon them.

This thought gave Yennenga renewed confidence, and she continued her frantic race, calling upon her grandfathers, grandmothers, and great-grandparents, both on her father's and mother's sides. After a while, she knew that although she might be alone with her horse in appearance, in truth she felt the presence of her ancestors who rode beside her, protecting and guiding her. She let their wisdom flood her mind; she was now certain that nothing bad could happen to her. She felt safe.

In the morning, back in the kingdom, when Tipgo got up and moved the braided mat that served as the door to her hut, she saw the traveling bird perched on one of the branches of the mango tree adjacent to her yard. She immediately understood the message: this bird always announced the departure or return of a person whom one missed. She quickly muttered a few prayers and thanked mother nature for the sign. Then, she hurried to wash her face and clean her teeth with her favorite toothpick. She wanted to be ready before the first patient came.

Chapter 8

Coincidence or Destiny

I don't think that anything happens by coincidence.... No one is here by accident.... Everyone who crosses our path has a message for us. Otherwise, they would have taken another path, or left earlier or later. The fact that these people are here means that they are here for some reason.

—James Redfield, *The Celestine Prophecy*

After riding all night and part of the day, the princess found herself in a vast clearing in the middle of the bush in an unknown land far from Gambaga where her exhausted horse finally stopped. The sun was already high, and activity had resumed in the few surrounding villages.

In this clearing there was a solitary hut; it was very welcoming and built not far from the path. Here lived a young elephant hunter named Riale. Before the era of colonization, there were many elephant hunters in the region of the Boussance, an ethnic group in southern Burkina Faso in West Africa.

Riale, whose name means "the one who eats everything," was also of royal descent. Indeed, he was the son of a Malinke ruler. He had been ousted from the succession by one of his brothers. Disappointed and a little humiliated, he had withdrawn into the forest to live as a hermit, far from the demands of royalty.

On the day Princess Yennenga found herself in the clearing, Riale had left his house at dawn to go hunting, and he had just returned. He was tired and a little disappointed because the hunt had not lived up to his expectations. He had spent most of the day in the forest looking but had returned home empty-handed, as he had the previous three days. His immediate concern was to find something to eat and then to reclaim the hours of sleep he had missed. As he warmed up the remnants of his previous day's meal, which he had carefully set aside, he thought about his hunt and what he might do differently over the next few days. His supply of smoked meat was beginning to run low and, if the hunt continued as it had, he would have to resurrect his fishing skills in order to survive.

He had learned the basics of fishing and hunting at a young age, but he had been naturally more drawn to hunting. Hunting offered him an opportunity to come into contact with the natural environment, to soak up its beauty, to marvel at its complexity, to understand its fragility. He was able to sniff out the trail of elephants at distance. He was never impatient and did it with real passion.

As an animal, the elephant had a unique sense of where to find water. This animal was always close to water holes but, in recent months, water holes were scarce due to a lack of rain, making it difficult for elephant hunters like Riale.

Elephants were hunted for their meat and for the ivory from their tusks. Despite his great passion for hunting, Riale never forgot that, when killing an animal, respect for traditions meant that the primary purpose was for food. The remaining parts of the animal's body were to be used either for clothing or for making various objects. Nothing was to be wasted; everything was to be transformed.

As a skilled hunter, Riale had learned to respect and understand nature. From experience, he knew that when we are honest and generous with nature, it always returns the favor. But it is nature that chooses the moment. It always has the last word.

Riale was still lost in his thoughts when he heard the whinnying of a horse. Exhausted, he longed for rest and silence. But now a traveler had disturbed his peace. This was the last thing he needed!

Nevertheless, he left his hut to see how he could help this lost traveler. Riale's upbringing had taught him to open his door to the stranger, because humanity was like a big tree. As the saying goes, "The tree never refuses the shelter of its shade to the woodcutter." This means that we must give hospitality even to an enemy and receive this person in a suitable manner in our house.

Yennenga was also exhausted, but she remained cautious. At the sight of Riale coming out of the hut, she felt her warrior instincts quickly come to the surface. Ready to protect herself in case of an attack, she placed her hand firmly on her spear. From a distance, she watched the stranger with an air of suspicion. Riale was wearing an ochre-colored tunic made of cotton strips with very specific patterns. Yennenga knew at once that Riale was a hunter. Despite her fatigue, she noticed that he was a tall young man with a well-controlled and proud walk.

With a smile that he tried hard to make welcoming, Riale approached his unexpected visitor cautiously. The horse started neighing again. Yennenga knew horses well and knew that their response to any potential danger was to flee.

She had a special bond of trust with this white stallion. Just by his whinnying, she could tell if he was afraid, angry, or just happy. The stallion didn't seem to be afraid at all; his whinny was short, soft, and low: it was an expression of joy. It was a very pleasant sound that Yennenga was used to and enjoyed hearing. It was very reassuring to the princess—she felt confident.

Still, she was surprised to see that the stallion seemed to be familiar with the place. The horse reacted as if it knew Riale, as if they had met before. With a gentle gesture, Riale calmed the horse by giving it a few strokes. Seeing the visitor's exhaustion, he helped the stranger off the horse.

In accordance with the rules of etiquette, it was customary to first offer the stranger a drink before inquiring about the reason for their trip. Riale did just that; he seated Yennenga comfortably in the shade and offered her a calabash of fresh water from his clay pot.

After the refreshments, Yennenga kept a shy silence that made the atmosphere a little tense. Deep down, she was wondering how to introduce herself to this hunter without revealing her identity. As a hunter, Riale had probably already heard about King Nedega and his powerful army.

Indeed, Nedega's reputation went far beyond the borders of the kingdom. He was known as a great innovator and military leader who was able to resist the incursions of other kingdoms; he had even managed to unify several ethnic groups with his formidable army. He had outstanding warfare strategies that allowed him to impose deterrence and respect.

Finally, Riale broke the heavy silence by asking with his

deep voice, "What good wind brings you to this somewhat isolated place, young man?"

Riale's voice startled Yennenga who was lost in her thoughts.

"The wind of peace and peace only," she answered quickly, before shutting herself up again in silence.

Riale asked again, "You look exhausted and seem to have come a long way. How long have you been riding, and where do you come from?"

The code of conduct did not allow Riale to ask directly for the name of his visitor; this would be seen as disrespectful. Indeed, it was known that one should avoid pronouncing one's name in the middle of the forest for fear that the powers of evil might take it. Moreover, asking someone's name directly was like granting oneself a certain power over that person.

"I'm from the other side of the river," Yennenga replied vaguely. "I can't say exactly how many hours I've been on the road, but it's been quite a while. If you don't mind, I'd like to rest for a little bit and give my horse a break before continuing my route."

Riale noticed that his visitor did not want to give him much information about his origin. Did he have something to hide?

In any case, it was not the first time that he had welcomed people who preferred to remain anonymous; with time he had realized that this was sometimes a good thing. It saved him from getting involved in problems he didn't know how to solve.

Nevertheless, he began to really examine his visitor with attention. Their war dress as well as the horse's saddle had a certain peculiarity that seemed familiar to Riale, but he couldn't remember from which exact part of the country. The way his visitor stood physically and his precise head carriage with his chin almost parallel to the ground denoted a certain status.

Because of the newcomer's thin voice and apparent shyness, Riale thought he was dealing with a teenage boy lost in the forest. He had never seen a woman riding a horse before and therefore never suspected that his young visitor was, in fact, a beautiful young woman.

"There's no problem resting here. You are welcome to my humble abode. As it will soon be dark, it would be wise for you to resume your journey tomorrow. By the way, my name is Riale."

Yennenga thanked Riale with a nod but did not say a word. Riale had no problem declaring his identity; however, he was not surprised when his visitor did not do the same. He thought to himself that here was another poor rebellious teenager who might be running away from his parents because of the weight of tradition. Anyway, if this was the case, he would soon hear about it from the other hunters. He didn't want to make his guest more uncomfortable than necessary. He would not ask any more questions and would wait for his guest to spontaneously introduce himself. It was important for Riale to respect these codes of hospitality and politeness, especially since, as the starting point of communication, the introduction and greeting set the tone for the rest of the interaction.

Now, in the presence of an unexpected visitor, Riale hurriedly finished warming the meal. Then, he placed two earthenware plates in the center of the mat he had laid out under the shade of the large baobab tree located very close to the hut. The baobab's shady foliage provided enough protection from the scorching heat of the day, and it was also where Riale ate his meals and rested when it wasn't raining.

One of the plates contained okra in sauce; the other, a starchy paste of small millet. One would take a pinch of the millet and dip it in the sticky sauce before putting it in one's mouth. Yennenga observed the meal with some hesitance. She was not used to eating meals that were prepared and presented with so little care. Besides, even if she was hungry, her fatigue was much greater than her hunger. Out of courtesy to her host, the princess took a few bites of starch and apologized for her lack of appetite. A little embarrassed, Riale offered her some wild berries he had picked the day before, which she gratefully accepted. It took Riale only a few moments to finish the rest of the meal, which he washed down with a simple cup of water.

Riale's hut was made of banco, a clay mixed with water and crushed straw. The roof was proudly covered with millet thatch, an assemblage of plant stems. The interior was very simple. It was accessed through a rectangular door. The sun's rays barely penetrated it, and it included a bunk made of a wicker mat. His hunting weapons were in one corner, and a series of different baskets made of woven rods that contained kitchen utensils and provisions were on the opposite side. At the back, a clay pot was used to store and keep fresh water.

Riale settled Yennenga under his roof. Out of hospitality, he offered his visitor his hut, which was a more comfortable place to rest and quickly regain energy. Indeed, the banco was a good thermal insulator which allowed the house to remain cool during the heat of the day. Afterwards, Riale watered her horse and removed the horse's corks. But, before he went to rest himself, he made sure that his visitor would have something to eat before leaving later that evening. He lit a fire but had to blow on the branches because they did not burn. A black and acrid smoke arose. After a few minutes, the fire was lit, and Riale placed a mixture of smoked meat and vegetables to boil in a clay pot upon the fire. He added water and eventually reduced it to a thicker soup, like a stew. Usually, condiments, especially crushed oilseed almonds, were added to the dish at the very end of the cooking process. Riale liked lightly bound sauces with large wild nuts. He also liked lightly spiced dishes but, in consideration of his visitor, he decided to put aside the crushed chili pepper mixed with coarse salt, which he would serve alongside the meal.

When Riale finished cooking, it was already dusk. The sun now looked like a ball of fire that was disappearing into the depths of the horizon. Exhausted at the end of all these unexpected tasks, he went to lie down on the mat under the big baobab tree to rest for a few hours before his visitor woke up.

When Riale opened his eyes, it was already dark, but the

moon gave enough light to see by. Exhaustion had overwhelmed him. At the sight of the horse, he suddenly remembered that he had a visitor. Riale got up with difficulty and headed toward the hut, taking care to announce his arrival by clearing his throat. Seeing no sign of his visitor, Riale stopped at the entrance of the hut and had a quick look around. Since the hut was not well lit, he did not see much, but he did notice that his special guest was still lying down and seemed to be sleeping deeply. Yennenga was tired and slept soundly; she did not even notice Riale's presence.

The moon was round and shining beautifully, and Riale decided to spend the night under the stars and let his visitor enjoy a restorative rest. He would keep the meal he had prepared for tomorrow. He was not hungry himself because he had not yet fully digested the meal he had had in the afternoon. He felt compassion for the young traveler who looked lost and didn't seem to know where he was going. As he did any time he spent the night under the stars, Riale lit a fire nearby the concession to keep the wild animals away.

As usual, Riale woke up at dawn. He set about relighting the fire to warm the previous day's meal. Before leaving to hunt, he usually liked to have a hearty meal that would last him all day. He was absorbed in his task when he felt a presence; he stopped for a moment and raised his head in the direction of the hut.

The first rays of sunlight entering the hut had woken

Yennenga. She got up, but she was still a little dizzy. She had lost her sense of direction and time; she could hardly remember where she was. In the confusion, she came out of the hut without her male disguise, exposing a firm, refined body of many a man's dreams.

Riale was surprised when he discovered that his guest of honor was actually a young woman! He was somewhat baffled—not so much by the fact that his visitor was a woman, but rather by her exquisite beauty. He saw before him a sublime woman with perfect skin. She had a beautiful figure and long black hair that turned him inside out. She was radiant, with a very beautiful face, even in the morning.

After coming to his senses and recovering from the shock, Riale played it safe, wondering if this beautiful creature was a genie turned into a beautiful young woman. His memories as a young boy resurfaced, reminding him of the stories told around the wood fire that warned him to beware of the genies' ability to assume the race of ordinary humans. Instinctively, Riale began to recite incantations known to ward off non-human presences.

When she saw Riale, reality hit Yennenga hard. She remembered everything: the escape, the long ride, and Riale's hospitality. Only then did she realize that she was not wearing her disguise, but it was too late to turn back. She stood there, petrified.

After finishing his ritual and seeing that Yennenga was

still there, Riale was reassured and shared his surprise with his visitor.

"I am surprised that a woman can ride a horse so well," Riale said.

Faced with the shock of the surprise, Riale forgot the conventions and the code of politeness. He asked, "Who are you? What are the reasons for your trip?"

At first hesitant, Yennenga glanced at Riale, trying to judge how much she could trust him. She thought he had big eyes and a friendly face. Then, feeling that she could confide in him, the princess finally revealed her true identity and told him about her adventure.

Riale listened to her with both empathy and admiration. Being of royal descent himself, he understood Yennenga's experiences and her desire for freedom from royal obligations. Riale also told Yennenga his story of how he had left his family and gone into exile in the forest.

Riale would usually leave early in the morning for hunting. However, with Yennenga present, he lost all sense of time. He wanted to know everything about her and to take advantage of every moment of her visit. For today, the hunt would wait. Riale was over the moon just watching her smile. He was fascinated by this perfect being who seemed to come from somewhere else, from another world.

After washing up, he served the meal, which Yennenga enjoyed with great appetite. They spent most of the morning chatting. Riale fell under the spell of this beautiful and unusual warrior. He invited the princess to spend another night but, without saying it out loud, he secretly wished that she would stay forever. The story of the princess had awakened a desire in Riale to hug her, to comfort and protect her. After all, he too had had to desert his kingdom. But who would dare to touch the daughter of King Nedega without his permission?

For the next few days, Riale continued to sleep under the stars, giving Yennenga the privilege of sleeping in the hut. The princess was seduced by the cordiality, kindness, and charm of her host. Over the next few days, she transformed Riale's hut into a real house and cooked him delicious meals. The hunter was pleased to see that the princess was not only a beautiful girl with warrior skills, but also had extraordinary qualities of a housewife that any man would appreciate.

During the few days they spent together, they got to know each other and discovered that they had a lot in common; what united them was far greater than what separated them. The time they spent together brought them closer: they knew they were made for each other, and they decided to stay together.

Thus, Yennenga gave up her kingdom, her status of princess, and her military glory to build another destiny: that of a wife. From this encounter was born a union marked by the seal of fate. The young couple couldn't help but think about the singularity of their encounter and the many unanswered questions. How come the horse stopped right in front of Riale's hut? Was it by pure chance or the hand of fate?

This question brought the princess back to the memory of

her horse's whinny of joy at the sight of Riale. Yennenga also remembered how Grandmother Tipgo had once told her that, when the time came, she would leave the palace and let the horse guide her in the direction she needed to go to find the answers to her questions. At that time, this made no sense to her: the best riders would tell you that it is the rider who leads the horse, not the other way around. She hadn't bothered to ask more questions because she was convinced that Grandma Tipgo was starting to feel her age and was losing some of her logic.

Now, sitting in front of Riale, Yennenga realized that Tipgo's words made sense. She felt a lot of compassion and love for the lonely old woman who was often misunderstood, but whose words and actions were full of wisdom if one made the effort to deeply analyze them. Yennenga was flooded with an immense sense of gratitude for having had the privilege to spend time with her and to benefit from her knowledge and teachings over the years.

What had seemed unfair to Yennenga at the time—being forced to remain single—now seemed like a blessing. If her father had allowed her to marry, she would not have met Riale. If she had known that, she would not have been so upset and harsh with her father: she would have seen things very differently. Yennenga came to the conclusion that sometimes it takes years before you can look back and say that you are happy that something happened, that you can see how it made you stronger and wiser.

Nedega had done what he thought was right based on his knowledge, understanding, and awareness. Even if she did not agree with some of his decisions, she understood that he had done his best.

Riale, on the other hand, realized the blessing of having been ousted from royalty. He didn't know it when he left the royal palace to come and occupy that piece of land. But now he understood that everything has a meaning and that often we do not always understand it when things happen. But there is no coincidence!

After months of living together, Yennenga discovered with great joy that she was pregnant. Nine months later, she gave birth to a beautiful boy, whom they named Ouedraogo, which means "stallion," to honor Yennenga's horse that had introduced her to Riale.

Chapter 9

Tipgo's Departure

In Africa, when an old person dies, a library burns to the ground.

—Hampâté Bâ

Yennenga's departure from the Kingdom of Gambaga also left a void in Tipgo's life. Over time, she had become very attached to the princess. Without admitting it, Tipgo suffered in silence, but it was a different kind of suffering. Yennenga's escape had not been a surprise to her. She wasn't worried at all because she knew that Yennenga was alive and that everything would be all right. Instead, she felt nostalgic; she missed terribly their walks in the sacred forest. She enjoyed Yennenga's youth and candor, she loved her questions and pertinent remarks, and she liked to see her marvel when she learned something new. Yennenga was a special person; she stood out from the other girls by her intelligence, her curiosity, and her thirst to learn. She was true to herself and dared to dare while knowing her limits and remaining respectful.

Tipgo and the other traditional practitioners were the guarantors of the ancestral memory, the mastery of traditional medicine, and the celebration of rites in honor of the ancestors. Therefore, she and the others also had a duty to make sure that this knowledge would not disappear with them when they left this world. Indeed, the transmission of knowledge through the generations was done through the extraordinary use of memory and speech.

This transmission of ancestral heritage had a sacred dimension; for Tipgo, it was more than a duty—it was a priestly duty.

The choice of who should have access to this precious knowledge and know-how was governed by certain procedures. The transmission of knowledge could be done in a filial way— i.e., from parent to child, as it had been in Tipgo's case—or it could be done outside of the family line. In all cases, the choice of the child to be initiated was subordinated to the interest and importance that the child gave to customs, integrity, and their capacity to live in harmony with the ancestral values. But even when the child met all these requirements, the most important thing was the call. Tipgo did not choose to be a traditional healer. The profession chose her; she felt the call and she answered.

Tipgo had the skill to identify the children who had this vocation, and she chose a young boy named Raogo. In general,

Raogo means "wood," but it also means "male." So the name Raogo symbolizes wood with all its attributes of solidity and righteousness.

Raogo had no mother, and his father was also a traditional healer. His father had married another woman after the death of Raogo's mother, but this wife was not very kind, especially toward Raogo.

Raogo was not very attracted to the activities of the boys of his age-group and, in order to escape the incessant criticism of his stepmother, he preferred the company of Tipgo who saw in this a sign of destiny to pass the baton and ensure the continuity of traditions and knowledge. She took Raogo under her wing and initiated him through education, daily teachings, tales, and advice.

Despite her advanced age, Tipgo was vigorous and still in full possession of her faculties. Since she had miraculously recovered from her great illness, she had never really fallen ill again: a little cold now and then, a little pain here and there, but nothing serious.

All the same, old age came with its luggage of physical weaknesses and limitations. Tipgo had no husband or children, so under the supervision of Queen Napoko, the women of the royal court made sure that Tipgo's house was immaculate and that she always wore clean clothes. They also took care of her daily meals.

It should be noted that respect for the elders was a very important traditional value; their white hair, crumpled hands, and wrinkled faces inspired consideration. These external signs were a reflection of their wisdom and, as it is well said, "What the elders see while sitting, the young ones standing on their toes won't see." This naturally resulted in a divine blessing for those who respected and cared for the elderly.

One day, just after the rainy season, Queen Napoko was asleep when she heard her name called. At first she thought she was dreaming, but when she paid attention she recognized the voice. Because of Tipgo's advanced age, a little girl would sleep in her hut in case she needed help in the middle of the night. So, how come Tipgo was there so early in the morning? A little worried, Napoko rushed to the door, wondering if it was the little girl who had a problem. It was true that Tipgo sometimes stopped by the queen's hut to say hello and have a little chat, but never at such an early hour.

She quickly pulled across the woven wicker structure that served as her door and saw Tipgo looking better than ever. It was still a little dark, but she could see her face clearly through the gloom.

Tipgo knew that Napoko would be worried about her visit, so she hurried to reassure her. "I'm fine Napoko. I just came to say goodbye because I'm leaving."

The queen knew immediately what she meant but did not believe a word of it. Tipgo saw death as a continuation of life in another dimension—a bit like the beginning of a new life. Therefore, she always talked about departure. Napoko remembered that when Tigpo was told about the death of a person, she always corrected the account by saying that the person was just gone and that there was no need to make a fuss.

There was nothing about Tipgo's condition that suggested that this was the end for her. She looked good and had a good appetite. In fact, Napoko had noticed that lately the dishes that were served to her came back almost empty.

In the face of Napoko's silence, Tipgo continued, "I thank you for your kindness toward me. You have considered me as a mother and, for that, may you be rewarded here on Earth as well as in the hereafter."

Tipgo paused, cleared her throat, and continued. "Don't worry about Yennenga; when the time comes, she will return to Gambaga, but I would like you to keep this information to yourself. And, most importantly, don't try to force this to happen because it would be a waste of time. Everything has its time, and there is a time for everything."

Tipgo held out her hand to Napoka as a farewell, and Napoka gently shook the frail hand while genuflecting as a sign of respect. Then Tipgo, with her hesitant walk, quietly returned to her hut under the incredulous gaze of Napoko.

This unusual visit completely disoriented Napoko and took away all her desire to sleep. She decided to get ready and go about her business earlier than usual. She was on duty that day for the King and, as usual, she would make sure that everything was perfect.

That morning in the bush, Yennenga woke up earlier than usual, and the first thought that came to her mind was the name of Grandmother Tipgo. For a moment she had a strange feeling, as if Tipgo was present in the hut with her. It was still quite early, and Riale was still asleep; she did not want to wake him up by making noise. She lay there but could not get back to sleep. She had a heavy feeling as if someone had put a weight on her chest. She couldn't wait for the sun to rise, because she thought that a little activity would make the discomfort disappear. However, this discomfort persisted throughout the day, sometimes accompanied by flashes of memories of Grandma Tipgo.

A few hours later, activity had resumed in Gambaga. The little girl who spent the nights with Tipgo got up, washed herself, and prepared the calabash of water for Tipgo as usual. But Tipgo stayed in bed much longer than usual. A woman came with her ailing child to consult with Tipgo; since Tipgo was still asleep, the girl asked her to come back later. However, the woman knew that Tipgo was always an early riser, and she wanted to make sure that everything was fine. She asked the little girl to inform Tipgo of her presence. The girl went into the hut and tried to wake Tipgo by shaking her lightly and calling her several times—"Grandma, Grandma, Grandma"—but there was only silence. She knew something was wrong and ran as fast as her little legs would carry her to alert Queen Napoko.

Tipgo had tiptoed away.

Chapter 10

The King's Pardon

Forgiveness does not change the past, but it does enlarge the future.

—Paul Lewis Boese

After the princess was reported missing, Nedega had never been the same. He ordered a search of the whole country. Delegations were sent to all neighboring regions and even to enemy territories to find the missing princess. But it was in vain; Yennenga remained untraceable, as if she had miraculously vanished.

Grief-stricken, the king began to neglect his kingdom. His pride and self-respect had been offended; his expectations and dreams, scorned. More than anything, he had lost someone who meant a lot to him. He sank into a deep grief and lost his taste for life.

Weary of years of fruitless searching, Gambaga mourned her precious warrior and princess. Thinking that they were doing the right thing, some advisers suggested to the king to think about organizing a funeral, but Nedega did not want to hear about it. He could not resign himself to the idea that his beloved daughter was no longer of this world. He clung, like a hunter to his talisman, to the predictions of old Tipgo, who had assured him that the princess was still alive and that the king would know in due course. Of course, he had pressed Tipgo with questions to find out more, but had been unsuccessful.

Tipgo had felt compassion for this old man. She understood his pain and confusion. She could feel his pain because she knew what it meant to lose a loved one. She said to him, "Nedega, some things are beyond our control, and sometimes the best thing to do is to accept the circumstances and surrender to the divine will. In the divine organization, everything is timed. So, we must give time to time, because if something is meant to happen, it will happen, no matter what."

Meanwhile, in the bush, little Ouedraogo was growing up well and had inherited the qualities of both his parents: intelligence, skill, and courage. His mother taught him horseback riding and the principles of warfare, while his father taught him the basics of hunting large animals such as elephants.

He became a boy his parents were proud of. Looking at him, Yennenga felt nostalgic about her childhood. According to Gambaga traditional customs, the first son of a princess should be raised in her father's family until he grows up. Yennenga also felt the need to reconnect with her family, to let them know she was fine and to introduce her son to them. But she feared rejection above all else. She had not abided by her father's desire to one day see her lead the kingdom, and she didn't know how her people would react. Now, looking back, she could see the full extent and gravity of her escape. As a parent herself, she could feel the worry and pain that her parents had endured all those years.

She was grateful to her father, who had disregarded tradition and allowed her to fulfill her childhood dream of riding horses and leading the royal army. Later, as she grew older, her childhood dream had changed. While she had wanted to take a different path than the one traditionally assigned to girls, later she had had another dream, that of every young woman: to be in love, to marry, and to become a mother. Could she blame her father for not understanding that her dream had changed, evolved over the years?

Yennenga longed to return to Gambaga to see her parents and friends, but she was apprehensive; she thought she might not be welcome. After all, she had abandoned them. She would have liked to tell them in person that she was sorry she had hurt their feelings. But that was not possible. Given the seriousness of her offense, according to tradition she would have to go through an intermediary to ask for forgiveness; to go before the king herself would be disrespectful and would guarantee that she would be banished from the kingdom forever. If Yennenga had remained in Gambaga, one of her uncles would have had the heavy responsibility of asking the king for forgiveness on her behalf. Riale could not be charged with this responsibility as he had no official status according to the tradition. There was only one option left: Ouedraogo, her son.

Despite the complexity of the situation, Yennenga decided to send Ouedraogo to his grandfather, Nedega, when he entered his teens. She told herself that no matter how much pain and resentment the people of the kingdom felt, they would not be able to resist the sight of an innocent young boy. In doing so, the fugitive and repentant princess had two missions: first, to make amends for the fact she had abandoned her kingdom and to be reconciled with her father; and second, to hear from her parents and to inform them that she was still alive.

The princess had a fervent desire to be reconciled with her father. Ouedraogo became the emissary who would go to meet the king to obtain his forgiveness. Because of the joking relationship between grandfather and grandson, which allowed for some discretions such as teasing, Yennenga secretly hoped that this aspect of the tradition would make it easier for Ouedraogo to be welcomed in Gambaga.

Indeed, this very special relationship between grandfather and grandson, governed by a code of jokes, also included the precepts of non-aggression, mutual assistance, respect, and solidarity, thus preserving the minimum of civility and respect, even in the event of a dispute. Besides, what grandfather could remain indifferent to a wonderful boy like Ouedraogo?

Finally, a day for departure was decided upon. Before his journey, Yennenga gave her son instructions: "Go find King

Nedega in his kingdom. He is my father. Therefore, he is your grandfather. He loved me very much, and I ran away. You will give him my news, and you will ask him for forgiveness on my behalf. When you come back, you will tell me in return if he has forgiven me and if he has welcomed you."

Growing up, Ouedraogo had always known from his parents that royal blood ran in his veins. Riale and Yennenga had not failed to tell him where they came from because they knew that it was important for Ouedraogo to have landmarks; it was important for him to know where he came from in order to better determine the next steps on his path.

Ouedraogo, at a young age, asked his mother, "If my grandfather loved you so much, why did you run away?"

Yennenga was taken aback and remained silent for a moment. She thought of the best possible answer. Knowing her son and his insight, she should have expected such a question and not been caught off guard. She smiled fondly at him and said, "Your grandfather is a great king. He loved me very much, but he loved his people more. The interests of the kingdom came first and that is what every good king should do. He wanted the best warrior he could trust as the leader of the royal army and that person was me. But I didn't want to be the head of the army. I just wanted to get married and have a wonderful son like you."

Ouedraogo's face lit up with a smile at this last sentence.

Then Yennenga said, "When I left Gambaga, I didn't know that I would have the chance to meet a wonderful person like your father. I encourage you to live with passion and to fight for what is important to you, because luck favors the one who dares."

Ouedraogo stared at his mother, trying to digest her words as best he could.

Riale accompanied Ouedraogo almost to the entrance of the kingdom.

Arriving in Gambaga late in the evening, Ouedraogo requested an audience with the king, as was the protocol. However, he did not declare his full identity; he just gave his name as Ouedraogo. He was told that he could see the king the next day because it was already getting late. In the meantime, he was the king's guest, and a hut was prepared for him for the night.

The next day, in accordance with protocol, Ouedraogo waited patiently for his turn to see the king. At the sight of the boy, Nedega was seized by an intense emotion. Without the boy even saying a word, he recognized in him the face of his daughter, whom he had not seen for many years. As they say, blood cannot lie; Nedega understood immediately that this visit had something to do with his daughter.

Indeed, Ouedraogo introduced himself as the son of Yennenga, Princess of Gambaga, and Prince Riale, and explained the reason for his visit. The king did not hide his curiosity and wanted to know everything. He listened with interest to the story of Yennenga's journey, of her encounter and life with Riale, and the birth of Ouedraogo.

The joy and emotion that overwhelmed the old man at the sight of his grandson was indescribable. Nedega was a great king and the head of a powerful kingdom, but at that very moment, all that did not matter. He was a human being, a father, and a grandfather.

Even though he was deeply touched, he did not want to let anything show; but it was difficult for him to contain himself given the circumstances. Indeed, according to the etiquette, a king should not let himself become too emotional, to the point of forgetting his social rank and his duty. And Nedega did his best not to deviate from this principle. Instead, he felt a mixture of relief and frustration: relief because his daughter was alive and he had a grandson, and frustration because Yennenga had kept silent all these years and was living with a man without Nedega's consent.

Nedega was very happy to meet his grandson. As he listened to Ouedraogo's story, Nedega recalled Yennenga's entire childhood. He could see her when she was just a little girl riding on horseback. But Yennenga was no longer the curious little girl who made old Tipgo laugh with her clumsy questions. Now she was a wife and mother to a wonderful boy.

The king had every reason to be angry at his daughter Yennenga, who had been alive and well all these years but who had never bothered to send any news. Yet, his joy overcame his anger at not having heard from his daughter, because he had a heart overflowing with love for her, and that love could not coexist with anger, bitterness, or resentment. The presence of one led to the disappearance of the other, just as the presence of light led to the disappearance of darkness. And this could only lead to forgiveness.

Nedega had now come to the end of his suffering: he stopped hoping that the past could have been different.

That night, in the silence of his heart, the king forgave himself for having wanted to change fate and forgave his daughter for leaving Gambaga. Peace and happiness once again lived at the royal palace. With forgiveness, bruised hearts healed, old quarrels and grudges were forgotten, and yesterday's enemies became friends. Everything seemed to be reborn into a new life.

The next day, the sun seemed to rise earlier than usual in Gambaga. The air was fresh and the atmosphere more welcoming.

The king summoned the elders and notables of the kingdom. "I intend to forgive the princess for her misbehavior, and I invite all of you to follow in my footsteps and let yourselves be guided by the voice of wisdom. I also ask you not to consider my act as a proof of weakness toward my daughter. The fact that I forgive her does not mean that I agree with the harm done, nor does it mean that I minimize its severity; far from it. The mistake Yennenga made is not erasable. We suffered from it, even though it can be explained."

The king had spoken with a calm and serious voice. It was no longer the voice of authority, but the voice of love and forgiveness. The tenderness of this powerful and intelligent man deeply touched the elders of the kingdom. The ruler was publicly performing an act of compassion, forgiveness, and love, which reflected humility, harmony, and authentic power. This was a powerful example and symbol for the people of the kingdom.

The oldest of the wise men of the kingdom spoke up to add, "The transgression of customs is wrong, but not irreparable. Human life is worth saving despite evil, as it is evil that is rejected—one never rejects a fellow human being."

The whole group of wise men nodded their heads in agreement.

Even though the king held no resentment toward his daughter, he had a responsibility to follow the customs and rules. The wrong done could not be forgotten or erased, but it could be made right. Princess Yennenga had committed a serious offense by leaving the kingdom. Her fault was twofold because, not only had she turned her back on her people, her union with the fallen Prince Riale was not in accordance with traditional customs. The king had not legally given his daughter in marriage.

According to tradition, marriage was a union between two families rather than between two individuals. For both man and woman, it was the only privileged setting for procreation. Therefore, a woman who became pregnant without being formally married, according to customs, was considered a humiliation for her parents. It was necessary to repair this offense. The first step was to consult the ancestors again for guidance.

Since old Tipgo had gone to join the ancestors, her replacement Raogo was put in charge of the sacrificial ceremonies to obtain the blessing of the ancestors and pave the way for Yennenga's return to Gambaga.

After imploring the blessing and protection of the ancestors and making all the customary sacrifices, the king said to his grandson, "You bring me a great consolation at the end of my life, and you will thank your mother for that."

Afterwards, an escort was sent to fetch Riale and Yennenga from their lovely forest. Yennenga's first gesture upon arriving in Gambaga was to kneel with a bowed head before the king, the dignitaries, and some of the elders of the kingdom, and then to express her sincere apologies.

The sign of Princess Yennenga's reconciliation with the Kingdom of Gambaga was marked by the sharing of the kola of peace. In Gambaga, kola nuts were often used in ceremonies and rituals and in all the important events of life: weddings, births, and funerals. In the case of conflict, the significance of the kola nut was twofold.

The fruit has a very bitter taste, but once chewed well it becomes a little sweeter. In Gambaga, the bitterness represented evil, and the sweetness symbolized peace. As a result, the kola was distributed generously to all the inhabitants of the kingdom as a sign of reconciliation and peace. By accepting the kola of peace, they agreed to turn a page on the painful past.

The king and queen were very moved to see their daughter again. The old man was so happy; he thought that only death would allow him to see his beloved daughter again. Emotion was palpable in the air. In front of her father, Yennenga could not contain the tears that ran down her cheeks. She could see the effect of the years on her father and also the effect of the grief of losing his beloved daughter in a mysterious way. She felt guilt. She felt that she had been selfish toward this man who had given her life and loved her with passion. Nevertheless, her departure from Gambaga had been necessary for her own well-being, because she would have been unable to fulfill her dream of being a wife and mother. Yennenga approached the king and gently kissed his feet. With complete sincerity, she asked for his forgiveness. But for the king there was nothing more to forgive. Exceptionally, the king rose from his throne as his subject stood before him, and he slowly lifted up Yennenga and spoke to her in a low voice so that only she could hear.

"You are forgiven, my daughter, and you are welcome to your home in Gambaga."

By this Nedega also meant, "I am sorry that I did not understand you, that I did not take your wishes into consideration." Knowing that Yennenga got his strong character from him, he knew that he might have done the same thing under the same circumstances, with the same information; surely he would not have done better.

Overcome with emotion, Yennenga kept her head down. It was at this moment that one of the old women present intoned a cry of victory. The return of the princess to Gambaga gave rise to warm rejoicing and festivities that lasted several days.

The royal couple even accepted Riale as their son-in-law. Thus, their unofficial union had to be turned into an official relationship. Some members of Riale's family came to Gambaga to ask for Princess Yennenga's hand in marriage. They offered a symbolic dowry, which included kola, jewelry, livestock, and some elephant ivory that Riale had kept. Their union was celebrated with great pomp, and the habitants of the kingdom could not have asked for a more perfect moment to celebrate the return of their princess.

When the celebrations were over, Nedega asked the couple to stay in Gambaga. But Yennenga preferred to follow her husband, who wanted to stay in his chosen environment, away from the pressure and obligations of royalty.

As for Ouedraogo, his destiny had just taken a new turn. He stayed with his grandfather to perfect his education as a man and a prince. As the only child in his grandparent's house and having known only wilderness and solitude, Ouedraogo enjoyed his lively life in the kingdom.

Chapter 11

The Future Belongs to Those Who See Possibilities

The size of your dreams must always exceed your current ability to achieve them. If your dreams don't scare you they are not big enough.

—Ellen Johnson Sirleaf

As an adult, Ouedraogo chose to leave Gambaga and move to his birthplace in the Boussance region. His royal education was complete. With his youth and determination, he saw the many possibilities that lay ahead. He could have chosen to stay with his grandfather and enjoy a peaceful and serene royal existence; the patriarchal system made him belong more to the family of his father than to that of his mother and, according to custom, he was almost the last in the order of succession to the throne. As a result, he would not have had to worry about bearing the burden of the responsibilities of army leader.

Ouedraogo had great confidence in himself and his potential; his worldview transcended the boundaries of the Kingdom of Gambaga. Already, one could see in him this vocation to gather, to unite, and to lead. He had an aura that seemed to give him an ascendancy over others. His creative drive, his ability to anticipate what seemed unpredictable to most people, and the greatness of his ideas made him a natural leader.

The Gambaga region was becoming overpopulated, and there was not enough land for the new generation of young men who wanted to have a piece of land and start a family. Ouedraogo managed to convince some of his friends to take the opportunity of his departure to leave their native region and found a new colony.

When he departed, in addition to entrusting him with hundreds of subjects and an escort of horsemen, the king gave him horses, oxen, goats, cows, a herd of sheep, and much gold.

Ouedraogo and his young army subsequently conquered several territories in the Boussance region, located in the south of present-day Burkina Faso. This young community constituted the first Mossi Kingdom. And this first kingdom was named Tenkodogo, which means "the old land." The word "Mossi," (originally called "Morho-si" in Bambara, one of the national languages of Mali) means "many men" and came from a speech made by Riale:

"I came alone to this part of the country. Now I have a wife, and I will have many offspring."

In saying this, Riale was referring to the offspring he had with Yennenga, and the kingdoms they created which went beyond his small forest in the region of the Boussance.

The new kingdom created by Ouedraogo was thus called Morosi, which, by distortion, became Mossi. Thus, it was the meeting of the Dagomba and the Boussance that gave birth to the Mossi people.

Yennenga lived long years of happiness with her companion Riale. After many peaceful years with him, she died in her beloved forest. Her remains were taken to Gambaga, where her people gave her a royal funeral.

Princess Yennenga ended her journey in the same place where, one morning before the rainy season, she had unknowingly left to meet love on her white stallion.

The grave of Yennenga became an object of deep veneration and a place of pilgrimage frequented by several generations of Mossi.

Chapter 12

Yennenga: The Wife and Mother

Open your arms to change, but don't let go of your values.

—Dalai Lama XIV

Although born with the privilege of being a princess and having the support of her father, Yennenga had dreams and pursued them to the end. However, her interests changed and evolved over time.

As a young girl, her dream was to ride a horse like the boys in the kingdom, and she was able to achieve it with the support of her father, who had to defy tradition. As she grew older, Yennenga had a more traditional dream. She wanted to marry and have children, but her father was adamant that she would remain at the head of his army for a time, and then she would marry whomever he chose and believed to be the right match.

From that moment on, Yennenga took her courage in both her hands and decided to leave the kingdom for the unknown.

She made a decision that took her life in a completely different direction.

In her quest for freedom and the pursuit of her dream, her parents suffered, and her people were disappointed. There was frustration and sadness. It was a matter of choice, and she chose to follow the path she thought was best for her rather than fulfill the king's dream.

Then, Yennenga showed the importance she placed on family ties by reconnecting with her father. It was with deep humility and great hope that she sent her son before the king to ask for forgiveness—forgiveness for the pain she caused and for her father's broken expectations, though these outcomes had not been her intention. She did not regret her choice to leave; she regretted the fact that it had caused so much pain, and she did her best to repair what was repairable.

In the past, traditional Mossi society was generally more restrictive because of various prohibitions and customs that affected all individuals in society, especially women. Habits and customs constituted the frame of reference that qualified and sanctioned positive or negative behaviors. Indeed, sanctions for disobedience could lead to a collective condemnation.

Respect for tradition was a quasi-divine veneration. Disobedience of tradition was tantamount to flouting the ancestors. Exclusion was the ultimate punishment and equivalent to social death. Yennenga achieved a feat that remains a major challenge, even today, in Mossi society: Without her parents' knowledge, she lived alone with a man in the forest for several years with whom she had a child out of wedlock—yet she managed to remain a respectable and respected woman. The seemingly unforgivable act of having a child outside the sacred framework of marriage was forgiven, not because what had happened became acceptable, but simply out of love. King Nedega had to put his ego aside and risk being seen as a weak king by his people. This love of Nedega for his daughter translated into unconditional acceptance. Even if life had separated them, even if there were wounds, love—stronger than anything—was able to repair what had been broken.

Yennenga lived in an environment where women had little choice in their destiny. But through determination, courage, and action, she forged her own path. She understood that she had a very important role to play in her own emancipation and assumed her responsibilities. It is true that sometimes the world can seem to be very complex and finding the purpose, meaning, and strength to pursue one's dreams can seem overwhelming. We all experience fear in life: fear of failure, fear of ridicule, fear of the unknown. These fears sometimes prevent us from growing and moving forward because we don't dare to act.

Yet, Yennenga's journey shows that when we can go beyond what we can see, taste, touch, hear, and smell, and perceive the world with the intelligence of our hearts and act in spite of the fear, that is when we are at our full potential and can accomplish almost anything. Yennenga went beyond her five senses, followed her instincts, and made fear her ally. She trusted the unknown by listening to her intuition, that internal compass.

Although Yennenga is often portrayed as a warrior—a rebel on a prancing horse with a spear in one hand—she was above all a gentle and loving woman and a devoted mother who preferred a peaceful life as a hermit to the life of a princess, warrior, and leader of the royal army.

She showed that the emancipation of women is not about wanting things to be complicated or different, or to be the equivalent of a man: It's simply about being able to make your own choices and taking responsibility for them.

Despite her innate talent, Yennenga had to train and put her heart into becoming the talented warrior that the royal army needed. Even with her father's support, Yennenga had to deal with criticisms and questions from the people of the kingdom. At one point, she had to face the most powerful person in the kingdom: her father, the king. Beyond her talent and privileges, Yennenga was a determined woman who, by working hard, earned the respect of society, her father, and the soldiers.

Yennenga defied social pressures to live a life as a young girl and woman that was different from the expectations of her community and traditions. Her actions and the values that guided her are of great importance even today. If we take the time to analyze them, these values remain universal tools that can help everyone, women and men, to live the most fulfilling life possible.

EPILOGUE

Everything can be taken from a man but one thing: the last of human freedoms—to choose one's attitude in any given set of circumstances, to choose one's own way.

—Victor Emil Frankl

Like Yennenga, during our lives we all face trials. Everyone experiences difficult times—some more than others, for sure—and no one is exempted. Life presents us with challenges of all kinds, regardless of our advantages: money, intelligence, beauty, social status, etc. None of these are guarantees of an easy and peaceful life. Challenges are an integral part of life. They lead us to make choices and our life unfolds according to the choices we make. We make choices that seem insignificant at first, but that can influence our lives in incredible ways.

Sometimes these choices can impact the lives of others and, even more broadly, they can define the fate of an entire people.

Such was the case with the courageous Yennenga, whose

choice to leave her kingdom led to the birth of the Mossi people. She is a true representation of a determined, brave, and independent-minded woman—the origin of the creation of the first Mossi Kingdom.

Yennenga's journey shows us that life's events are not random; we are spiritual beings with a specific purpose in this human experience that is life.

Certainly, life presents challenges, but if we allow ourselves to be guided by our intuition, that internal and innate compass within each of us; if we listen to the desires of our inner being; and if we make choices based on love and hope, everything becomes possible.

In laying the foundation for this new Mossi empire, Ouedraogo paved the way for the famous lineage of Moro Naba, the King of the Mossi. It is Ouedraogo who is considered the founder of the Mossi Kingdom, but let us not forget that without the courage of his mother nothing would have happened.

Ouedraogo himself had three sons: Rawa, Zoungrana, and Diaba Lompo. According to other traditions, he had only two sons, Rawa and Zoungrana; Diaba Lompo was his cousin. Rawa moved to the north and created the Mossi Kingdom of Yatenga. His brother Zoungrana stayed with his father in Tenkodogo and had a son named Oubri who became the founder of the city of Ouagadougou. Diaba Lompo went east and founded the Gourmantche or Gourma dynasty. Although this last kingdom is not officially part of the Mossi empire, its history remains linked to the formation of the Mossi Kingdom resulting from the lineage of Yennenga, daughter of Nedega, King of Dagomba, and Queen Napoko.

These main kingdoms form the regions of present-day Burkina Faso: Ouagadougou, which is the current capital located in the center of the country; Yatenga, which borders Mali in the northwest; and the Gourma, which borders Benin and Togo in the southeast.

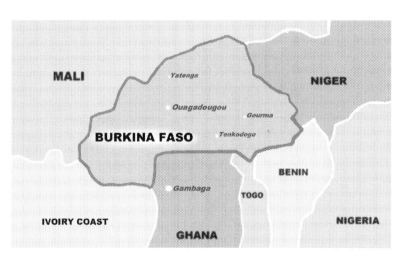

The Mossi, whose language is Moore, is one of the major ethnic groups in Burkina Faso, making up about 60% of the population (more than seven million inhabitants). In addition, the family name Ouedraogo is one of the most common family names in Burkina Faso.

Even today, the Moro Naba symbolizes traditional power in Burkinabe culture. The Mossi Kingdom has a highly structured organization. The Moro Naba holds political and religious power and is assisted by four ministers: the *ouidi-naba* or chief of the cavalry; the *gounga-naba* or chief of the infantry; the *larhale-naba* or chief of the royal tombs, customs, and traditions; and the *baloum-naba* who is the steward of the palace.

The current Moro Naba of the Mossi is the 37th sovereign descended from Ouedraogo, the son of Princess Yennenga. Together with his ministers, he represents the highest traditional authority and still holds a very important political influence in modern Burkina Faso.

Today, Yennenga is very present in the culture of Burkina Faso. For example, represented on the coat of arms, the national emblem of Burkina Faso, is the white stallion that guided the princess. Yennenga is also represented in batik dyes, sculptures, and bronze castings made by Burkinabe national craftsmen.

In the world of cinema, the most important prize of the Pan-African Film and Television Festival of Ouagadougou (FESPACO), which takes place every two years, is called "The Stallion of Yennenga" in recognition of this heroine's courage. The trophy of the Stallion of Yennenga, in gold, silver, or bronze, is the highest award given at this festival.

BIBLIOGRAPHY

Agora Africaine. "Yennenga, Queen, Warrior, Politician, Founder of the Mossi Kingdom and National Emblem of Burkina Faso. Africa with The World," 2020, http://www.black-feelings.com/accueil/detail-actualite/article/yennenga-reine-guerriere-politique-fondatrice-du-royaume-mossi-et-embleme-nationale-du-burkina-faso/.

Reines Heroines D'Afrique. "Yennenga-Founding Mother of The Mossi People," 2016, https://reinesheroinesdafrique.wordpress.com/2016/03/30/yennenga-mere-fondatrice-du-peuple-mossi/.

Ilboudo, Monique. "Le Politique, un Bastion Bien Gardé," in *Droit de Cité: Être Femme au Burkina*, 131. Éditions du Remue-Ménage, 2006.

Journet-Diallo, Odile. "Names of Ancestors, Names of Friends, Names of Derision: African Examples," *Spirale* 2001/3, 19: 51–60.

Paré, Marie-Eve. "The institutionalization of male migration among the Mossi. A study of a socio-cultural change in

Burkina Faso." Master's thesis, University of Montreal, 2009. https://papyrus.bib.umontreal.ca/xmlui/bitstream/handle/1866/4079/Par%c3%a9_Marie-Eve_2009_m%c3%a9moire.pdf?sequence=6&isAllowed=y.

Titinga Pacéré, Frédéric. *Ainsi On A Assassiné Tous Les Mossé*. Canada, Éditions Naaman, 1979.

UNESCO. "Women in African History," https://en.unesco.org/womeninafrica/yennega.

Vinel, Virginie. "Female Life Ages and Intergenerational Relations in Burkina Faso," *Le Portique* [online], 21, 2008, https://journals.openedition.org/leportique/1803.

Printed in the United States
by Baker & Taylor Publisher Services